cloverleaf books™

Our American Symbols

Can We Ring the Liberty Bell?

Martha E. H. Rustad

illustrated by **Kyle Poling**

M MILLBROOK PRESS · MINNEAPOLIS

For Maxine —M.E.H.R.

For Dad and Mom, Joanne and
Herman, Donna and Ned, and Eva
Jean and Jim
                            —K.P.

The image in this book is used with the permission of:
© Racheal Grazias/Shutterstock.com, p. 22.

Millbrook Press
A division of Lerner Publishing Group, Inc.
241 First Avenue North
Minneapolis, MN 55401 USA

For updated reading levels and more information, look up this
title at www.lernerbooks.com.

Main body text set in Slappy Inline 18/28.
Typeface provided by T26.

Library of Congress Cataloging-in-Publication Data

Rustad, Martha E. H. (Martha Elizabeth Hillman), 1975-
    Can we ring the Liberty Bell? / by Martha E. H. Rustad ;
  illustrated by Kyle Poling.
        pages   cm. — (Cloverleaf Books: our American
  symbols)
    Includes index.
    ISBN 978-1-4677-2137-0 (lib. bdg. : alk. paper)
    ISBN 978-1-4677-4769-1 (eBook)
    1. Liberty Bell—Juvenile literature. 2. Philadelphia (Pa.)—
  Buildings, structures, etc.—Juvenile literature. I. Poling, Kyle,
  illustrator. II. Title.
  F158.8.I3R87 2015
  974.8'11—dc23   2013043419

Manufactured in the United States of America
1 – BP – 7/15/14

TABLE OF CONTENTS

Chapter One

A Visit to the Liberty Bell

Today is a **field trip** day! Our teacher says we are going to see a famous American symbol.

Melissa says, "My big brother plays the cymbals in band!"

Mr. Chen smiles. "Not the instrument. Here the word *symbol* means 'something that stands for something else.'"

The Liberty Bell hangs in Philadelphia, Pennsylvania. A copy of the Liberty Bell hangs in every US state. Most states keep their bell in or near the state capitol building.

"Like a heart means love!" says Amira.

"Yes!" says Mr. Chen. "Can anyone name a symbol of America?"

"The flag!" says Benjamin.

"The bald eagle!" says Simon.

"Good thinking," our teacher says. "Today we are going to see the **Liberty Bell**. *Liberty* is another word for '*freedom*.'"

5

We ride the bus to **Independence National Historic Park.** Ranger Marcela meets us outside the **Liberty Bell Center.**

"Welcome!" she says. "I have a riddle for you. The Liberty Bell doesn't make a sound. So how can we help it ring?"

"Shake it?" asks Thomas.

"No, we can't shake it," answers Ranger Marcela.

If you want to visit the Liberty Bell, you'll have to spit out your gum and candy. Sticky foods are not allowed near the bell!

"Then I have no idea!" says Lyla.

"Keep thinking about my riddle. I'll tell you more about the bell," our guide says.

Chapter Two

A Bell to Share the News

"Look behind me," Ranger Marcela says. "During the 1700s, that building was called the **Pennsylvania State House.**"

We learn that people in Pennsylvania's government worked in the State House.

Ranger Marcela says, "Let's talk about communication. How do we learn news today?"

"Watch TV!" says Ryan.

Mr. Chen says, "I check my phone."

It took nineteen years to build the Pennsylvania State House. That's because the government kept running out of money to pay workers to build it!

"Listen to the radio," Sylvia says.

Our guide asks, "Did people have phones, radios, or TVs in the 1700s?"

"No!" we all say.

We learn that **bells rang** to tell people there was **news**. Then people went to the State House to find out what was happening.

We follow our guide into the museum inside the **Liberty Bell Center**. She tells us that the **State House** needed a new bell in **1751**.

"Workers in England made a bell that year," Ranger Marcela says. "It arrived in Pennsylvania in 1752. But it **cracked** the first time it was rung."

"It cracked right away?" says Jaden.

"Yes, it was too **brittle**. So workers here melted the bell down. They made a new bell with the metal," she tells us. "It was hung in the State House."

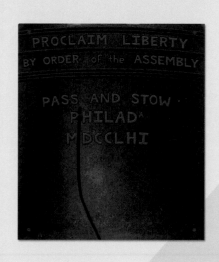

"I ask you . . . to adopt the principles proclaimed by yourselves, by your revolutionary fathers, and by the old bell in Independence Hall . . ."

-Frederick Douglass, 1866

The Liberty Bell is made mostly of copper. It also contains tin, lead, zinc, arsenic, gold, and silver.

We walk through the museum.

"When the bell was made, **Pennsylvania** was part of **Great Britain**," Ranger Marcela says. "Many people living in America wanted their own country. They wanted to be **free** to make their **own laws**."

We learn that our country's founders signed two important papers in the State House.

The Declaration of Independence said America wanted to be its own country. It was signed in **1776**. **The Constitution** is a set of rules for our government. It was signed in **1787**.

Ranger Marcela adds, "Because these papers were signed in the State House, today it is called **Independence Hall**."

"Take a look at this X-ray," Ranger Marcela says.
"It shows what happened to the bell in 1846."

"I had an X-ray when I broke my arm!" says Zack.

We all look at the big X-ray of the bell. We can
see a crack.

"The bell cracked and broke when it rang for **George Washington's birthday.** Does anyone know who that was?"

"Yes! He was our **first president**," answers Delia.

"Correct! He died in **1799**. We still remember his birthday," our guide says. "The bell rang for the last time on that day in **1846**."

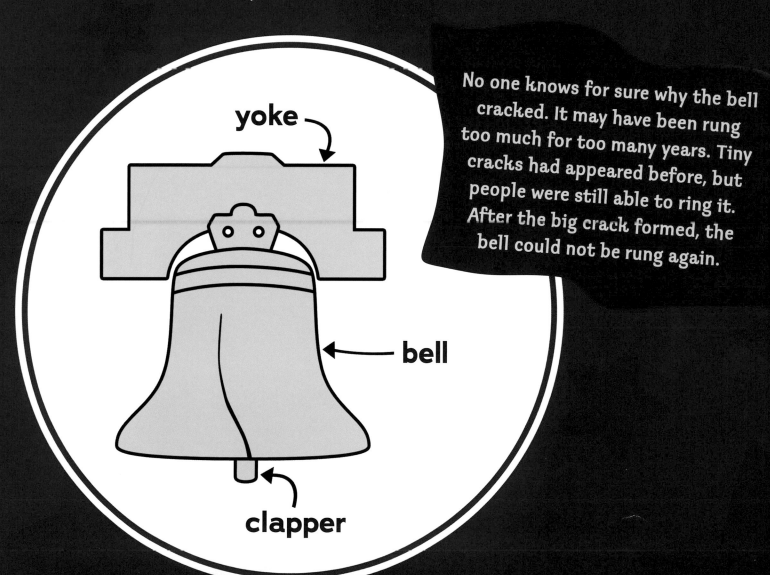

No one knows for sure why the bell cracked. It may have been rung too much for too many years. Tiny cracks had appeared before, but people were still able to ring it. After the big crack formed, the bell could not be rung again.

Chapter Three

A Symbol of Liberty

At last, we see the bell!

"Why do we call it the **Liberty Bell**?" asks Mr. Chen.

"Good question," Ranger Marcela says.

"Look closely at the top."

"I see the word *LIBERTY* right there!" says Nikolas.

"Yes," our guide says. "It says **proclaim liberty**.
Proclaim means 'to tell everyone about something.'

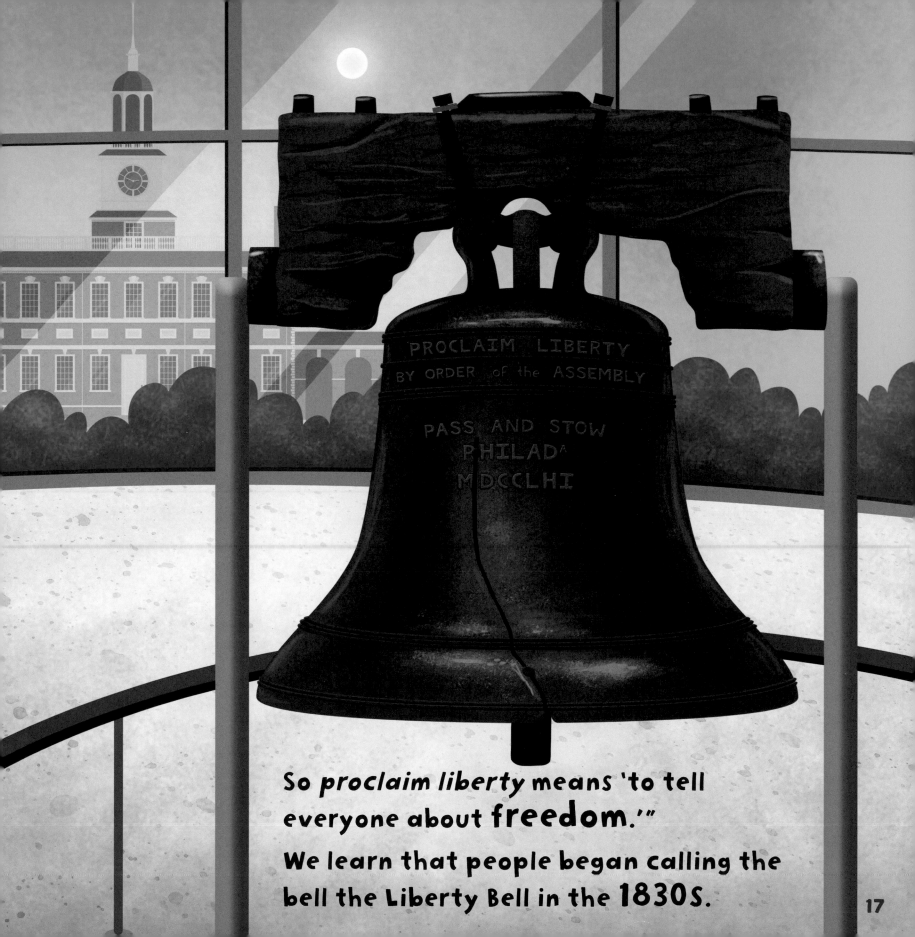

So *proclaim liberty* means 'to tell everyone about **freedom**.'"

We learn that people began calling the bell the Liberty Bell in the **1830s.**

Chapter Four

Ringing for Freedom

"Can we ring the Liberty Bell?" asks Diana.

"Sorry," says Ranger Marcela. "Remember, the Liberty Bell is broken. It doesn't ring anymore."

Mia says, "But your riddle said we can help it ring. How can we ring a bell that doesn't work anymore?"

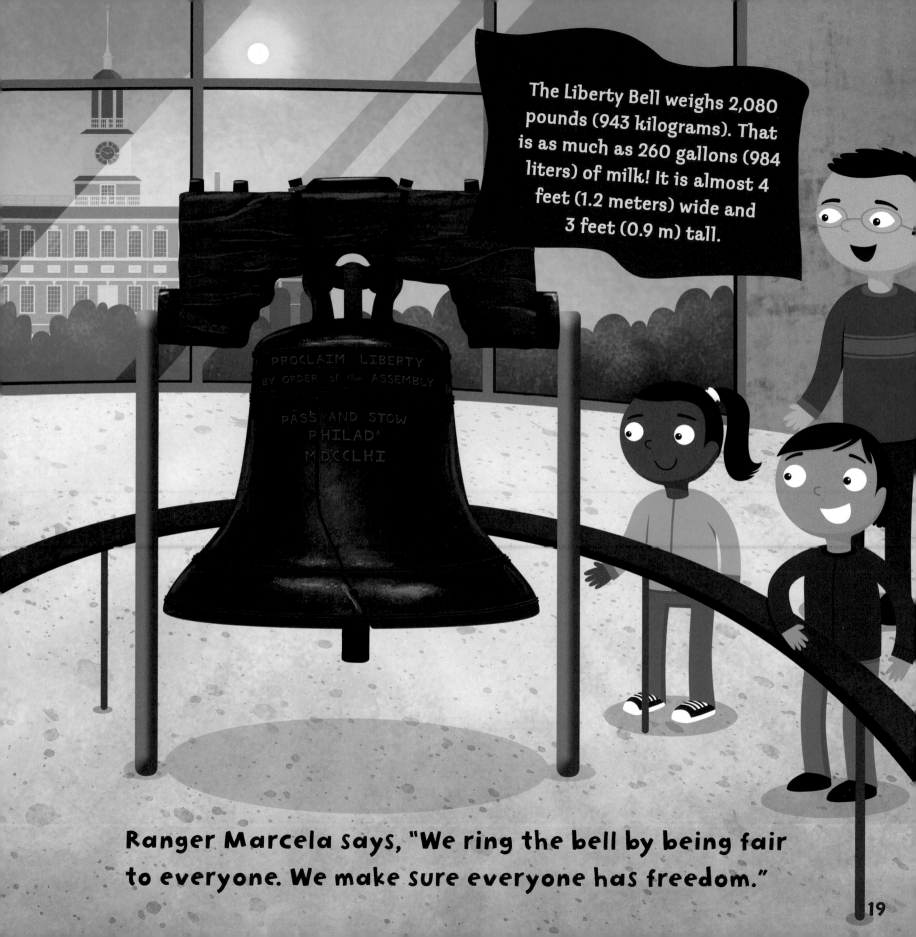

The Liberty Bell weighs 2,080 pounds (943 kilograms). That is as much as 260 gallons (984 liters) of milk! It is almost 4 feet (1.2 meters) wide and 3 feet (0.9 m) tall.

Ranger Marcela says, "We ring the bell by being fair to everyone. We make sure everyone has freedom."

Our field trip is almost over.

"What do we say to our guide?" Mr. Chen asks.

"Thank you, Ranger Marcela!" we
say together.

Back at school, we hear the bell ring at the end of the day.

"That bell rings for your freedom from school!" our teacher jokes.

We all run around on the playground. It's **good** to be **free!**

Every year, relatives of the country's founders tap the Liberty Bell on July 4. People also tap the bell in January on Martin Luther King Jr. Day. They do this to honor King's work for freedom for all people.

Hide the Liberty Bell!

Americans hid the Liberty Bell from British soldiers during the Revolutionary War. They feared the enemy would melt it down to make cannons. They hid the bell under the floorboards of a church in Allentown, Pennsylvania. Where would you hide the Liberty Bell?

What You Need:

large sheets of paper or tag board
tape

ruler or tape measure
scissors
crayons, markers, or paint

1) Measure and mark off the dimensions of the Liberty Bell on your paper or tag board. It is 4 feet (1.2 m) wide and 3 feet (0.9 m) tall. You might need to tape pieces of paper or tagboard together to make a piece that's large enough.

2) Following the example *(right)*, draw and decorate a picture of the Liberty Bell. Don't forget to draw the crack! It is about 25 inches (63 centimeters) long. Cut out your bell.

3) Divide into groups. Take turns hiding and finding your Liberty Bell.

GLOSSARY

brittle: weak and easy to break

capitol: a building where leaders meet to make laws

clapper: a metal piece that hangs down inside a bell and hits the sides of the bell to ring it

communication: ways to tell news

copper: a reddish-brown metal

founder: a person who starts something, such as a country or a company

liberty: freedom

museum: a building that stores and shows items from history, science, or art

symbol: something that stands for something else

X-ray: a picture of the inside of something

yoke: a piece of wood from which a bell hangs

The Liberty Bell hangs in Philadelphia, Pennsylvania.

BOOKS

Eldridge, Alison, and Stephen Eldridge. *The Liberty Bell: An American Symbol.*
Berkeley Heights, NJ: Enslow Elementary, 2012.
Learn fun facts about the Liberty Bell from this nonfiction book.

Figley, Marty Rhodes. *Saving the Liberty Bell.* Minneapolis: Millbrook Press, 2005.
A young boy and his father must save the bell from British soldiers during the Revolutionary
War in this story.

Harris, Nancy. *The Liberty Bell.* Chicago: Heinemann Library, 2008.
Find out more about the Liberty Bell and why it is a great American symbol.

WEBSITES

How the Liberty Bell May Have Sounded
http://www.nps.gov/inde/thelibertybellsounds.htm
Listen to the bell before and after it cracked.

Liberty Bell Center
http://www.nps.gov/inde/liberty-bell-center.htm
Read about the Liberty Bell and the Liberty Bell Center.

Liberty Bell Timeline
http://www.ushistory.org/libertybell/timeline.html
See important dates for the Liberty Bell.

LERNER 𝓮 SOURCE™
Expand learning beyond the printed book. Download free, complementary educational resources for this book from our website, www.lerneresource.com.